REVIEWS

"'Let's hear it for history's little people,' Pamela Cranston writes, surely eliciting a smile from the reader. Actually, the admonition epitomizes something deeper in her work: the recovery of people otherwise ignored, their recreation through images both tender and firm. Resurrecting them, she pleads, 'let my words be to you / like the green earth cherishing.' Like burgeoning life for us, too, fortunate guests in *The House of Metaphor* she so blessedly builds."

—Sofia M. Starnes
Virginia Poet Laureate Emerita,
author of *The Consequence of Moonlight*

"Pamela Cranston's wonderful, accessible poems are a temple of metaphor. Her juxtapositions and never clichéd similes surprise and delight. Her penetrating insights engage the reader. Allusion to classical English poetry deepens the resonance of the work's heart-truths. These are poems to revel in and ponder. To hurry through them would be like eating a box of fancy chocolates at one go. Don't."

—Bonnie Thurston
Author of *Saint Mary of Egypt*

"Early in life, nature called to Pamela Cranston and sang. These poems show she has an ear for it, a studied gaze—an unhurried heart. She listens to people too, no one stereotyped, each incomparable, sent to her as if a poem. Cranston has the gift of paying attention, close and rapt, and then translates what she hears into poetry, helping us to hear and see—to become more human, more alive, somehow in the heart of God."

—Bishop John S. Thornton
Co-founder of the Hospice of Marin, author of *Moon and Fog*

"Although she will deny it, Pamela Cranston is a mystic. For me, a mystic is someone who sees surfaces as rubble to dig through to find the truth, or truths, someone deeply in touch with depth(s), not just an onlooker, or even surveyor, but an inhabitant of what is most true, hence sacred. As someone who often finds it difficult to find light, I celebrate the luminescence of the poems in *The House of Metaphor*."

—Tim Vivian
Professor Emeritus of Religious Studies,
California State University Bakersfield

The House of
METAPHOR

Also by Pamela Cranston

Poetry
Coming to Treeline: Adirondack Poems
Searching for Nova Albion

Nonfiction
An Eccentric English Journey (Limited Edition)
Clergy Wellness and Mutual Ministry
Love Was His Meaning: An Introduction to Julian of Norwich
A Spiritual Journey with John Donne

Fiction
The Madonna Murders

For my husband Ed, with much love and gratitude.
With you, home is not just a house
but wherever I am with you.

"Unless you are at home in the metaphor . . .
you are not safe anywhere."

—Robert Frost, *Education by Poetry*

"Metaphor shakes things up, giving us everything from
Shakespeare to scientific discovery in the process. The mind
is a plastic snow dome, the most beautiful, most interesting,
and most itself, when, as Elvis put it, it's all shook up. And
metaphor keeps the mind shaking, rattling and rolling, long
after Elvis has left the building."

—James Geary, *I Is an Other: The Secret Life of Metaphor*
and How It Shapes the Way We See the World

CONTENTS

II

III
TREADING ON HOLY GROUND: HOSPICE POEMS

PERMISSIONS

My thanks to the editors of the following journals and publications in which poems from this book have previously appeared, some in different form:

The Anglican Theological Review: "Lines Inspired by Bach's Last Fugue," "The Hiding Place"

Bibliophilos: "At the Villa"

Crosswinds Poetry Journal: "Bell Ringers of Bredwardine"

Journal of Pastoral Care & Counseling: "Fooling Death," "Impatient for Death," "Blossoming into Light," "Kaddish Poem," "Brain Tumor," "Elegy for Lyndsey"

Pensive: A Global Journal of Spirituality and the Arts: "Dead Letter Drop"

Please Call Me: "Washing Hands with Florence Nightingale"

When Sickness Heals: The Place of Religious Belief in Healthcare. Siroj Sorajjakool: "Kaddish Poem"

The Windhover: "Crossing the Line"

"The House of Metaphor" won an honorable mention from the Poetry Society of Virginia's 2021 Edgar Allan Poe Memorial Prize, judged by Gregory Donovan.

ACKNOWLEDGMENTS

The author is grateful to the following people: The Revs. Pam Higgins, Connie Hartquist Jacobs, Zoila Schoenbrun, the Rev. Dr. Tim Vivian, and Patrice Haan for reading these poems over many months and for their continual support and encouragement.

I am especially indebted to my editor, Suzanne Underwood Rhodes, for her skill at wielding her editorial pruning shears with wisdom, grace, tact, humor, and professional skill.

Finally, none of this would be possible without the humor, constant support, and abiding love of my husband, Edward Cranston.

I

WASHING HANDS WITH FLORENCE NIGHTINGALE

No one dreamed she'd come back
from retirement, but there she is
in her long black gown, white apron,
and small lace cap, pulling up
the guards over her straight sleeves
and making sure the towels are clean.

She is standing by the sink, stern
as ever, never giving an excuse
nor taking one. I'm by her side
learning to wash my hands
like a nurse. She watches,
hawk-eyed, scrutinizing
my every move.

I let the warm water gush
from the faucet as I rub my palms
and fingers together, feeling
soapy lather slip and slide
over my hands. Then I use a brush
to scrub under my nails, washing
the cuticles and the white half-moons
rising in my nails' pink skies.

People usually do this for twenty seconds
by singing "Happy Birthday" twice,
which she doesn't know and I don't like,
so we compromise. When she washes

she sings the Doxology. I sing
"Ob-La-Di, Ob-La-Da," which she times
with a stopwatch pinned
to the chest of her white apron.

Next, she makes me clean
the counter tops with Clorox wipes
and lets them air-dry to kill the germs.
She inspects them as if she can see
the microbes dying one by one.

She tells me to do all this
three times before I get it right
as if she were a Zen master teaching
the art of sitting or the Way of Tea.
As if my life depended upon it
(which it does). As if it could save
the Crimean army or even
the whole world.

After this, she says,
Let's have tea and crumpets,
then we can say evening prayer.
Of course, I say, I'll put the kettle on,
bring out my best china and serve
the heartiest Assam tea.
The barest smile flashes
across her face: Yes,
but we're not done yet.

Then she marches me down
the hall to clean the toilets.

MY MUSE

He's a young man with flowing hair
and Chopin hands. When his fingertips
touch my words, they turn to chimes.

He is pale as moonlight from staying indoors
helping poets all day. At night,
he disappears like a monk
in a cowl of darkness, drenched
in the music of soaring stars, so
he has high expectations.

When I ask him for help
he catches the essence of poems
like fireflies in a jar, sneaks
behind me unseen, and whispers
scarce words in my inner ear.

Each word he speaks
crackles with its own music
like Ben Franklin's key
struck by lightning.

THE HOUSE OF METAPHOR

"Unless you are at home in the metaphor . . .
you are not safe anywhere."
—Robert Frost, *Education by Poetry*

A young poet knocks at the door
of the house of metaphor.
He's the new apprentice.
Palladian columns and a round pediment
adorn this brick house. Tucked
beneath the wings of St. Paul's
along Paternoster Row, it's a study
in restraint—a quiet invocation.

A secretary in low heels takes him
by the print shop rife with metallic ink,
the crank and thump of Star Wheel
and Albion presses—past matrices of lead
and brass type, punch cutters, hand molds,
etched copper plates, ink balls, struts and slugs,
and the bindery brimming with reams of paper
halved and creased by slick bone-folders.

Next floor up they view the library,
its mahogany shelves stuffed with books.
Cases teem with displays
of living metaphors: Yeats's
glowing seeds of fire, Dickinson's
blue and yellow thing with feathers,
and Plath's brown bag filled with God.

5

Last, they climb to the top floor
bright with windows. A man stands
at a compositor's desk. He is bearded
and wears glasses. A green visor
crowns his bald head; a leather apron
hangs from his neck. Instead
of setting type, his job is to find
unborn metaphors.

He sorts through a pile
of letters and broken words
then links them together—
long-lost twins now conjoined.
He shoots packets of metaphors
by pneumatic tube up to the clouds
where poets throughout the world
pluck, harvest, and sift them.
The young man asks,
What are metaphors good for?
His boss smiles a knowing smile
and says, *They change you,*
maybe they change your heart.
Maybe even the world.

Digging through the pile, the boss
finds and links a new metaphor:
Organ—a piano with wings.
He holds it to the light
to prove it's not counterfeit.
He hands it to his new apprentice.
Put it in a packet and send it up.
Soon you'll be making metaphors too.

ABANDONED

"I agree with Valéry: 'A poem is never finished;
it is only abandoned.'"
—W. H. Auden

On a summer day,
a red wheelbarrow:
an abandoned poem
with not a chicken in sight.

As you guessed, it belonged
to William Carlos Williams
but there was no way
I could return it to him,
as he lies quite dead and buried
in the solid dirt of Hillside Cemetery,
Lyndhurst, New Jersey.

I wonder, what other poems
lie hidden, tossed aside
by weary or impatient poets?
Many poems find refuge in attics
or books. Most are left to litter
the alleys of chain-link towns
or wash out to sea
like millions of plastic bags
in the great Pacific garbage patch.

So I hunted for lost poems
and soon spotted Shelly's skylark
trilling songs in a tree
and down by the rusty port,
Hopkins's great hulk,
the wreck of the *Deutschland*,
portside salvage, its deck
stress-stroked and sunk
by the storm's sharp lash.

Over in the junk yard,
I found e. e. cummings's
once brand-new car,
its carburetor and clutch
completely busted,
and a few condoms
lying on the back seat.

After several hours
of poking around, I saw
my project would soon overwhelm,
so I headed home. But then,
Mary Oliver's grasshopper
turned up, sunning itself
on my front step,
twitching its queer, disjointed legs.

PHANTOM MAIL

All the mail morgues have died except one
in Atlanta. Jetsam of lost mail piles in plastic bins.
Once, the post office stored lost letters, rings,
locks of hair, Model T tires, glasses and rosaries,
boxes of snuff, poker chips, and even bat wings.
Now they hold toys and DVDs, body parts,
marijuana, queen bees, and postcards sent to no one.

What I want is a mailbox for letters to the dead.
I'd use a fountain pen, India ink, and white silky paper.
Of course, I'd write to my favorite authors: Hopkins,
Blythe, and Merton, Herbert and C. S. Lewis.
If I felt in a playful mood, I'd write Groucho
and Thurber, E. B. White, and Flannery O'Connor.

With luck, if this mail drop has extended service,
I'd send prayers to saints like Gandhi, Julian
of Norwich, and Martin Luther King Jr.
And I'd write a genius or two: Bach and Jung,
Einstein and Planck, full of perplexing questions
they can now finally answer.

The letter I'd most want to get is from my long
dead brother, each page written with his crabbed
left-handed scrawl as if inked by scarabs
crawling up a rope. I'd gladly decrypt each page
to read his sturdy prose again, his gentle wit.
How he loved the views beyond the rocky cairns!

So now I pen my lonesome words to him:
How goes the climb? What pinnacle
have you touched?
But my stars, you should see
your granddaughters!
Please write soon.

PIG LAZARUS OR THE END OF BAR-B-QUE

*(In 2019, scientists made news when they revived brain cells from
dead pigs.)*

If they succeed, how will we ever
sleep at night? Who can brush away
the thought of one unlucky pig
waking up in the lab on a night
of the living dead, Frankenpig,
all bristled, rolling and wriggling
his barrel body, snuffling snout,
albino eyes, fully alive from the tips
of his pink ears to his corkscrew tail?

I imagine the astonished faces
of his fellow swine as they watch him
trot back to life in his dainty cloven boots,
a porcine Lazarus or Jesus, to save them.
No more slaughterhouse for them,
no more groans or flipping out,
no more running in circles, crying
their high-pitched squeals of terror.

Are we prepared to pay the price
for this? Don't they know
that whatever rises up
from the dead comes back
to haunt us?

SINGING POTATOES

"I can hear a song in any overboiled elderly spud."
—W. H. Auden

Auden loved them twice a day
even though they smell
like boiled shirts when cooked.

Of course, the idea of them singing
is ridiculous, but if we dispense
with anatomy, anything's possible.

If stones can speak and stars sing,
why not spuds?

Maybe at first, they hum,
mumbling like blind-eyed moles
digging with five-fingered spades
their crooked subways underground.

But when they rise from their clotted graves,
who wouldn't want to burst into song?

Not arias or serenades,
but something simple, down
to earth—melancholy
as a bald Irish bard plucking

his harp by the fire, singing
sweet, bitter songs
about famine and blight,

grubbing from barren ground
the bare root of hope.

ROAD INSTRUCTIONS

First, bust your way
out of whatever cocoon
you've been living in.

Second, shed your snaky skin
and learn to live raw for a while.

Third, hammer the steel box
surrounding your heart
and crack it open.

Fourth, empty the sack
of frozen tears
you've been hiding in the dark.

Fifth, bring home the puppy
of happiness but make sure
it's house trained.

Six, turn off your GPS
and learn from geese
how to fly home.

Seven, steal your neighbor's shoes
and walk in them until they feel
like they're yours.

Eight, when you're chasing
your muse don't forget
the people you've left behind.

Nine, love whatever valley
you're in—few things grow
on mountain tops.

Ten, hide an extra coin
from the Ferryman—
who knows, you might need it.

TAKING TOLL

Sometimes our dead ends
are destinations
that save us
from each other.

Like those times
in the name of life
when we need to get lost.

So lost, any port
or lifeline will do—
when the crooked hand of pain
is the kindest friend we have.

Like a drunk who drives
to the tollgate,
stops,
climbs out of his car,
walks into the toll booth and calls,
Honey, I'm home.

BEAVER MEADOW FALLS

All day the waterfall spreads her white sheets
   like a washer woman over crags of wet rock,
      flush against the flanks of cliffs,
         reckless, splashing, bending where stone

has been rucked, raised by granite thrusts.
   Her effluence flows ceaselessly—
      music healing and feeding the strings
         of my heart. I melt into silence.

Its clean force gushes
   over smooth rock, washing
      the psychic grime
         of my work world away.

Here, bright rugs of wet moss shine, lit
   by green flames from within. Fronds
      of maidenhair fern billow and shake
         their tiny ladders in the wind.

Think of it! To behold a blade of grass,
   a pool of water, sunlight
      blinking through the branches. Bliss
         to touch the mystery of matter.

A POEM FOR CONNOR MCLAUGHLIN

(2004 – 2016)

Up the rutted trail on a cloudy day
to the base of Roaring Brook Falls,
we startled upon a memorial
nailed to a tree by the brook,
a homemade house-shaped block
with slant roof and thick gold heart
etched with the word "Connor"
and a photo of a sun-streaked boy.

Later, I read that he and his uncle
had stopped on a whim to see the Falls,
hike to the base, admire its ancient cleft.
Above, a rock dislodged, plunged
a hundred feet, and, as if aimed, struck
the luckless boy. His uncle yelled
and rushed to shield but was too late.
He died where water once washed
my brother's ashes, scattered
on a cloudy day like this.

Back on our porch close to the Falls,
I mourn for a boy I never knew.
At dusk, a doe and her fawn stroll
into our yard. She licks her wobbly child
from head to hoof, then they step
through tall ferns edging the road.
Cars whiz by.

They hesitate, wary—
I hold my breath.

MIXED FEELINGS ABOUT BATS

After lights out, mouse-eared, blind bags
of brown fur squeeze through chinks
in the eaves. They fly folding, unfolding
their tracery fans. Chirps ping
against my bedroom walls
like faint Geiger-counters.
They swoop and wheel around my room,
sweeping puffs of air, skimming
a hair's breadth from my sheet.

When I was young, one night, eek!
nine bats circled our living room—
a string of drunken birds,
a fleet of black-sailed ships.
Mother and I shrieked
in our nightgowns, wild
as witches. Brooms swatted
wooden beams, flying balls recoiled
and veered off the walls. They left
when we turned up the lights
and opened wide the two French doors.

These days, Adirondack bats
are almost extinct. Fungus-killed.
Good at snapping up unwanted bugs,
they serve as night-time Hoovers.
What will we do when they are gone?

The last few hang from their stirrups,
upside-down in icy caves,
sleeping their long winter sleep,
wrapped in thin leather cloaks
as if born wearing
their own shrouds.

THE LINCHPIN

When bees sleep in their papery nest,
the first bee clings to the top
of the conical hive as the second
grips its hind legs with its forefeet
from below, then the next bee
and the next, until a hundred

bees form a winged ladder
hanging down the sides
of waxy cubicles in the dark.
Does the first bee ever get any rest?
Who picks it to play this part?
Do they take turns? Does this bee,

with its black googly eyes, know
it has a cross to bear as it clings
to the crepe roof, its hairy hind legs
clutched by claws of a sleeping drone?

It prays to the God of bees not to let go.

THE HUNGRY HEART

A young doe, sleek,
   acorn-brown, trots
      down a dusty road then   slows
        to a procession of one.
She stops
   and eyes two fields
      thick with buttercup and lupine.
        One is close, the other   far.

She dithers, pondering
   where to dine.

I stop, put down
   my pen, and watch
   as she noses the air
      tasting its bouquet.

It happens every time—these divine arrests,
   whether it's a doe and her fawns
      nipping tufts of grass
        in our front yard

or a stag wearing
   a crown of velvet horns,
      majesty incarnate, strolling midday
        down our city street.

My world slows, then   stops
   as my hungry heart, waiting
     in its nest of ribs,
      is fed.

TWENTY-TWENTY VISION

The germ lurks
unseen
like a World War II navy mine,
exploding our daily grind
of buy and sell,
and sadly for too many,
our treasured lives.

Forced to live like cloistered monks
in our sorrowful time of plague,
will we learn the quiet joys
of Sabbath, how to build
better selves of clay
as we spin our potter's wheel?

But all is not lost. Everywhere,
the skies are blue again, and peacocks
trail their emerald fans in Dubai.
Cougars prowl the lanes of Santiago.
Shaggy long-horned goats
clop down Welsh cobbled streets.
Coyotes, bears, and deer roam
Yosemite at will, and mahouts
free elephants from their rusty chains.

This time, for once,
may our lonely windows
offer us a better view.

May this cosmic timeout
show us how to cherish
each other, teach us to be meek.

Maybe it's our last chance
for an earth to inherit.

MY GRANDFATHER'S TYPEWRITER

A sepia photo shows him toiling at his typewriter,
a 1930s Underwood, solid and black, with lyres etched
on top of two spools. The brown bowl of his pipe bobs
as his stubby fingers float above the keys, then strike.

Words bunch on the page like boxcars in the snow.
Sheets of *Gallant Dust* pile up in a box, telling
of foxtail pines and shallow soil bled gray by need,
and a poor planter's love for Gaya, the gypsy girl,

in the post-war South. Mark Twain knew the power
of mechanical print. Twain bought his Remington Model I
in 1874, so new he called it his "curiosity breeding little joker."
He knew how the smell of metal and ink gets the juices flowing,

how the QWERTY chrome keys cup your fingers like tiny saucers,
how the heavy feet almost merge with the desk. The hulk
doesn't budge even when you slide the belled carriage hard
or slap the hammer-slugs on the page coiled around the rubber roll.

Make no mistake, typewriters are strict taskmasters. Errors
aren't easily fixed. But keys on computers quickly wear out—
they abet verbal dysentery and sloppy thinking
while cyberspace lures you down bottomless holes.

My grandfather's framed photo sits firmly on my desk
and like his old Underwood issues its ultimatum:
Keep writing. Don't give up. And whatever you feel,
don't ever, ever quit.

MY PARENTS' WEDDING PHOTO, 1950

It's the usual black and white glossy—
the family gathered, dressed
in wedding best. My grandmother,
crowned with silver braids,
stands stately as a statue
in her low-cut gown and jewels.
She smiles fondly at the flower girl,
a celestial blonde, who's gazing
at the bride and groom
as if they're movie stars.

My father is blue-eyed and suave.
He wears white tie and tails,
holds a glass of champagne
and a cigarette in one hand.
He's smiling, my mother also,
Madonna-like, radiant in white.
I am there too, four months
hiding in the cave of her body,
behind her Easter lilies.

My grandfather, stout and bald,
stands beside her, scowling,
eyes shooting buckshot
at the photographer.

They don't know that I'll land
two months later, feet first,
cat-like into the world. Was I
impatient to start living
or bailing from a toxic womb?

Did they resent being pushed
so soon to parent? Was this
behind the booze and betrayals
beneath their social façade?
I never asked.

I barely survived my birth.
Luckier still to survive
the frozen tundra of childhood.

The gift they gave me
was resilience.
Like a plum tree, I learned
to blossom in winter.

WHAT WATER DOES

1

I escaped, a lone fledgling
from its nest. I must have opened
the garden gate and toddled down
the gravel drive but all I remember
is the slender path that hemmed
the shallow stream, the sun's surprise
dazzling the water, and the river
flashing its jewels.

I stepped thigh-deep into the downrush
to pluck a stone from the bottom,
felt the water sweep me downstream,
a fast-floating leaf.
I watched green arms of trees
that couldn't catch me pass by.
They filigreed the clouds
floating in their own blue deep.

The river flowed into a pond
and swallowed me in its black maw.
Monster boulders crouched in the murk.
I opened my mouth to breathe
underwater—too young
to know what water does.

2

Mother, I know, I know.
You were busy with my baby brother.
You never noticed I was gone
until the house grew hushed.
Frantic, you searched, shouting my name,
then faced the river that carried my distant cries.
You raced to the pond, saw me floating
on my back wailing in the water.

Sixty years on, each year you'd tell us
how you saved me from drowning.
And each year, I'd thank you
sincerely for saving my life.
But I wondered why
you needed to keep telling
the story, like a dog
gnawing a bone it can't bury.

Now, you've crossed
your own river and I realize,
perhaps my gratitude
wasn't enough.

Maybe you needed me
to lift you
out of your drowning guilt.
Maybe you really craved
my forgiveness.

I give it to you now,
even now.

UNCLE JACK, HOME FROM BOOT CAMP

My brother and I tumble into his room
on Ashley Road like adoring puppies
and watch him bend over the sink, scraping
white foam from his chin, then tap minty powder
from a tin of Pepsodent onto his toothbrush.

Next, calisthenics for all—jumping jacks
and touching toes ending with pushups.
He does ten with us both riding
on his back. We ride him up and down
like a dime store pony until he flops
on the floor with a grunt, sweating,
as we roll off shouting, "Let's do it again!"
But he says no and laughs
with that low-rumbling nicker of his.

But that's what he's done
for seventy years—carry us all.
His yearly calls and visits out West,
upscale restaurant splurges,
his wordless hand on my shoulder
when Mother died. Never telling
when love's burden was too heavy
to bear or that he knew
the secret of shifting the load.

THE HIDING PLACE

When I was ten, I found a cave
long abandoned by trolls
and stout-hearted hobbits.
Part of a large estate,
the cave was really a Quonset hut
covered with dirt and green sod
built inside a hill—a garden shed
in disguise. It boasted a handmade
wooden door, an eight-foot ceiling,
and a dirt floor made of hardpan.
The smell of pungent earth
filled this dark womb
and wrapped me in its warm snug.
Shovels, rakes, forks, and hoes
stood against the dank walls,
alert as sentries waiting for orders.
A hand-push lawn mower
rested in the corner. I stepped inside
and inhaled the rich mull of black marl,
the scent of cut grass still clinging
to the scythe's sharp blades. All
I wanted was to curl up like a corm
and take root there—to make a nest
like the mud wrens
who build their caves of wattle
and daub, laced with sticks,
fur, and sweet hay—to be like the birds

who never feel the hooked barb
of loneliness, who always know
where home is.

LEAVING CAMP

Girl Scout camp, 1959

I am eight, sun-bleached, runty.
I'm used to hopscotching up brooks
and sitting by woodland silent wells,
not latrines, swim drills, canvas tents,
or the forced jollity of crafts.
Tired of beaded cord bracelets
and clay pendants, I am ready
to go home.

In the parking lot I meet
the camp mascot, a black raven.
When his cold hooks grip
the soft branch of my arm,
I shape-shift into a tree and feel
rooted, centered, somehow known
by this dream sifter, harbinger
of the unknown, bringer of fire,
crux between worlds,
herald of death. Looking back,

Raven was portent—messenger
of my future life as priest
and hospice midwife.
In the snapshot, I smile
as if I'd swallowed a rainbow.

THE COPLAND SUITE

1

Hook Road, Bedford, New York, 1930

The lanky man from Brooklyn
with sprawling hands and receding hair
bends intensely over the keyboard
crunching chords. He strikes the keys
as if he hates pianos. His music
is dangerous, like hobnailed boots
and broken glass—a portent
of the coming war.

So perhaps it's a relief
when my father from next door,
(age seven, blonde with big ears)
wanders in for a visit. He sits
on the bench by the man
and gaily bangs out random notes.
The composer writes them down
on paper lined with staffs.

My father runs home
to show off his masterpiece.
We'll never know what happened
to this priceless ephemera.
Was it saved then lost?
Or trashed? I mean,

who knew that Aaron Copland
would turn out to be
Aaron Copland?

2

Tanglewood Festival, Lenox, Massachusetts, July 28, 1970

All night, stormy hooves canter
toward us trampling the wide horizon.
My parents and I have joined thousands
to mark Copland's seventieth birthday,
even as lashes of rain, like drovers,
push picnickers off
the great lawn into the Shed.
First, Copland's "Fanfare"—triumphant
brass notes slice the air like whips.
Next comes Bernstein's music. Loud applause
as Copland strides onstage, exuding light.
He faces the orchestra,
lifts his baton as if plucking lace,
and tears into "Candide" at sonic speed.

Then hoedowns and hymns
from "The Tender Land," with parts
so slow, you could see quarks move.
Last, as Tchaikovsky's "Romeo and Juliet"
swells, we hear sky-drums bang
even louder, like God
on the timpani.

The loudest clap comes just as Romeo
and Juliet climax, and we jump.
Everything else is a let-down,
like the end of a rodeo when the crowds,

the clowns, and the cowhands go home
and the horses sigh in sweet hay, resting
their heads, closing their dark eyes.

3

After the finale, after the rain,
I race backstage to see if the maestro
might appear, unsure if he'll come,
unsure if I'm even in the right place.
At last, he swoops through the door,
rushed on the wings of his black satin cape
but I am stunned speechless,
my mouth sewn shut.

He pauses, expecting a request
for an autograph, but all he sees
is a statue
locked in place.
He smiles, bemused,
then turns and strides away across the wet grass.

Wait, wait! There's so much I want to say!
How he rented our house on Hook Road
when my father was a boy,

how his music heals my heart
when it is sore.

But the moment has flown
like a bird from its cage,
like my father's gleeful notes.

FOOLING DEATH

Signs of my father's impending death
pester him daily like mosquitoes—
or shrapnel. The heavy luggage
of his body sags in his recliner.
He cradles his left arm
like a withered child,
milky eyes, dull tongue,
the mini-strokes that burst
like cherry bombs on the Fourth of July.

His turquoise iPad sings old songs
that echoed in his barracks. He plays
B. B. King's "Caldonia" over and over,
blows his harmonica with his good hand,
and shouts the lyrics to drive away
the dark that eats at him like rust.
It proves to him (and everyone else)
he's still alive. Tomorrow,
he will think of another trick.

MY FATHER'S LAST CHRISTMAS, 2016

In Santa Fe, flurries drift down on rabbit brush and sage.
Inside, my father sits bundled in his wheelchair
by a blinking Christmas tree.

Pale and tired, he tilts sideways.
Mistletoe hangs overhead on his lamp—
any excuse for a kiss.

He (and we) know this is his last Christmas,
but he does not speak of it.

He wears a red Santa hat and with his good hand
holds a leash leading to Thurston, the hound,
who sits compliant, sporting green antlers.

This is Dad's joke, marking the time Thurston
on his leash sent my father and his chariot
flying down the drive chasing a squirrel—
Dad's biggest thrill in months.

I'm here on the 25th, the first time
in thirty years. (Christmas for clergy
is always booked.)

Somewhere, a spotted owl spears the dark
with yellow eyes.

Swallowing is hard, my father barely eats;
he feasts on the warmth of family instead.
He who will be dead five days later

takes a glass of forbidden wine
and lifts it high in salute;
"Best Christmas ever!"

TIPPING POINT

Nature is tired
of being knocked around,
neglected and abused, like a girl
pushed hard against a wall
then taken for all she's worth.

Each year, she sends us
hundred-year floods, high tides,
tornadoes, fires, and droughts,
hoping we'll get the message.
But we never do.
So, she's fighting back.

She goes big and casts up
dead whales; a thousand dolphins
wash ashore. From Tampa
to Goodland, she flings her red scarf,
and life in the strangled sea dies.
What do we care?

This spring, she hit the ceiling.
Weather.com reported a cloud
of ladybugs eighty miles long.
Millions of millions flew—a swarm
of red coats, a giant car lot
of tiny VW bugs flying to Hesperia.

Next thing you know, thousands
of polar bears will step
off their cubes of ice to march
from Ketchikan to Tacoma.
If they could write,
they'd carry signs.

But will there be people left
to read them?

We, so smug in our conceit
that we're creation's kings,
are being mowed like grass
by a spiteful germ
that flaunts its crown.

A MURDER OF CROWS

Imagination is the door to the raven's house . . ."
Robert Bly, "The Dark Autumn Nights" from *My Sentence Was a
Thousand Years of Joy*

In the time of persimmons
hundreds of crows flew,
midnight at noon, soaring,
swooping, tumbling,
diving in barrel rolls
just for the fun of it.

In the time of crackling leaves
when earth was parched as paper,
they came. They fell from the sky
black as cinders, foretelling
the firestorm in Paradise
soon to come.

I watched as this conclave squawked
and wheeled around the oaks
searching for a place to roost,
the way dogs circle invisible beds
before flopping down
on their haunches to sleep.

Few know where crows hide their nests.
If you watch one build a nest,
you can bet it's a decoy.

They scavenge for trinkets:
paper clips, white buttons, chips
of glass, hoarding them
in the twisted thatch like gems
stashed in the dark
like plundered stars.

What omen do these bandits
carry on the wing as they build
their contrary world?

Tell me, where can I find
the key to their house?

FIRE IN PARADISE

Nestled between the breasts of canyons
carved by the relentless rush of Butte Creek
and the Feather River, the town of Paradise
smolders, ravaged by a ravenous flaming hydra.
Nothing is spared the licks of its countless
red tongues: trees, homes, stores, schools,
churches, and cars, even the town sign.

The firestorm burns one acre per second;
a tourniquet of toxins strangles the air.
Trees hurl chunks of hot coal at burning roofs.
People panic and flee their cars on foot,
clutching children or pets in their arms—
their heart's blood beating in their ashen mouths.

The fire is so big, it scorches
the bottom of clouds like tin pans.
The blowtorch from hell reaches so far
it solders the pearly gates; fire
almost sucks the streams arroyo-dry.
Leaves, like singed wings of angels
or scraps of gossamer, float off
into the copper sky. Charred limbs
of trees hang outstretched,
like dead men across time's horizon.

Meanwhile, the rebel angels laugh
and fly away, wearing red hats,
hunting for something else they can burn.

THE FIRST CIRCLE OF HELL

Thick smoke circles the house,
    a burglar prowling in a gray hoodie.
        It stakes out the place for days
            then sneaks under our doors
        and through the transom, setting off alarms—
    fire trucks come though the fire
burns a hundred miles away.

Smog claws at our lungs like spiteful cats.
    Twilight smothers our town in broad day.
        At noon, an orange disc hangs
            in the milky sky, a dim filament,
    a bad bulb from one of Edison's
failed experiments.

Far away, the town of Paradise
    lies under a sepia pall. Burnt-out homes
        lie gutted—open caskets of the dead
            whose ashes sift down like snow.
    When we inhale dense air,
the lost live again.

DARKNESS AT NOON

For two weeks, forest fires roared
up and down the West Coast
like a flaming dragon. We woke
one day to find its red-hot eye
glaring down at us in rage. Nothing
prepared us for the apocalyptic sky,

for the sepia pall of ash, smoke,
and fog that smothered the air
after the dragon ate the sun,
after a cosmic light-tech slipped
a filter over the clouds shading the bay,
the bridges, parks, shops, and homes.

Of course, it confused us all,
starting with the birds who failed
to broadcast their morning songs.
The streetlights never switched off.
People had to dress in the dark
and flip on their headlights at noon.

The sky turned pumpkin.
By noon at City Hall, it darkened
to a deep burnt umber, as if
we'd all left earth
to live under a Martian sky.

I had a chilling thought: what if this day
repeated over and over like Groundhog Day
and the sky never turned back blue?
What would this do to life on earth?
Let it sink in. There'd be no more sunsets
or shadows, just a dull brown light

killing the grasslands, the forests, and ferns,
snuffing the cows, the cornfields, and groves,
not to mention crashing the solar
and sunscreen industries. Instead of robins,
we'd see bats and owls all day
and even a nightingale or two.

And if by some miracle we adapted
(unlike dinosaurs) to this alien dusk,
would we become albinos or even
transparent as fish in the deepest dark sea?
What if we learned, like them,
to see more without light?

THE ASSASSIN

*(Sara Jane Moore attempted to assassinate President Gerald Ford
in San Francisco on September 22, 1975.)*

I was a tender chaplain at the county jail
when she donned her powder-blue trench coat
(she called it her assassination uniform),
pulled a .38 Special from her purse,
aimed at President Ford, and shot.

They took her to the Hall of Justice,
a concrete box with windows slit
like IBM punch cards.
Black inmates called it the Hall
of Just Us. The steel doors clanged.

Four cells, painted probate green, flanked
the rec room on the Women's side.
No TV. Stainless steel tables, a beat-up piano
with missing keys, a long row of plastic chairs
under an opaque window. Making my rounds,

I didn't know the brown-haired matron
until she said her name. Despite
the orange jumpsuit, she wore her class
like a string of fake pearls,
like the claim she hailed from ritzy Blackhawk
(exchanging one gated community for another.)

We had the Catholic Worker in common
yet she sized me up for the easy mark I was,
conning me for favors. Later I read
she shuffled personas like a deck of cards:

one day, a charming hostess serving tea,
and a rebel pushing revolution the next.
"The .38 would have made a nice, healthy hole
if I hadn't missed." The times we met,
she never mentioned the aliases

or the four children she left behind.
If people were flies, she'd pull off their wings—
each relationship a mutilation. Shrewd,
always defiant, something sour
seethed beneath her skin.

How was I to know
that everyone she met
came into her crosshairs?
I never felt the plug until I got home.

BARBWIRE BABY JESUS

Up from dirt floors and corrugated shacks
they come. They trek through scrubland

along the Camino de las Espinas
through catclaw, sage, and mesquite.

Spines grab their clothes, their skin
like fishhooks. They lie awake in ditches.

Sand fleas bite all night. "Coyotes"
cram them into trucks like boxed cigars.

Across the border, they put José,
Maria, and Jesús in steel cages

good only for dogs. Men stand
and stare for hours, each glance

a payload of despair and grief.
Boys lie listless on gym mats,

wrapped like baked potatoes
in silver thermal sheets.

ICE says, "We have nothing
but the best government specified care

and well-trained clinicians."
But no one gets toothpaste or a brush,

showers, or soap. Soiled toddlers
wail for hours, inconsolable.

Girls complain, *The hammer
in my heart hurts.*

After months apart, Maria
and Jesús finally unite.

He crawls away, afraid
to be touched. She stretches out

her arms, *But I'm your mother!*
He curls up in a corner and looks away.

AT ST. ANTHONY'S SOUP KITCHEN

Alone, age six, Mister Omnipotence
folds his arms against the world.
He slouches against the rail
in the soup line, a cowboy
at the roundup. He's wearing
a small leather jacket and swaggers
to ward off bullies. I bend down to him—
Can I help you? What's your name?

He recoils and looks frantically
for the door. His eyes
narrow with despair—
a bum of fifty.
*Look, will you please
leave me alone?!*

Nothing but his size
and the pink stuffed rabbit
he drags by one ear
tells his age.

COMING TO THE TABLE

I

1935 WPA Interview with Leroy Day:
A Former Slave from Georgia, Age 80
A Found Poem

I was born in Georgia,
I was there in slavery days.
My old Marster had an overseer
who whipped the people pretty rapid.

Old Marster, his name
was Joe Day, he was good to us.
They called him Judge Day.
He seemed to be a Christian man.
I never seen him whip nobody,
and never seen him have no dispute.
I tell you if he wasn't a Christian,
he sure looked like one.

I used to be strong; I done a heap
of work in my life. Cotton and corn
was the business. The white man
had the land and the money,
and we had to work
to get some of that money.
Since I become afflicted,
(I'm ruptured)
I can't do no work no more.

The fust man I ever seed killed
was one time a colored man's dog
got in another colored man's field
and ate his roasting ears.
It made him so mad he shot the dog
and then the man that owned the dog
killed the other man. I never did know
what the punishment was.

I remember when the Ku Klux
was right bad in Louisiana.
I never did see any—
I didn't *try* to see 'em.

I heard that they went to a schoolhouse
and broke up a Negro convention.
They called for a colored man named Peck
and when he come out, they killed him.
And one white man got killed.
They had a right smart scrummage.

After this, the colored people ran off
and went to Kansas.

I used to vote after freedom.
I voted Republican. Things got so
now everything is in politics.
Some votes because they want
their friends in office
and some don't take no interest.

I don't remember anything else.
If I had time to study,
I might think of something else.

II

LETTER TO A SLAVE
BY A SLAVE-OWNER'S DESCENDANT

"For sweetest things turn sourest by their deeds;
Lilies that fester smell far worse than weeds."
—William Shakespeare, Sonnet 94

Thank you for your kind words about my great-great-grandfather, Judge Joseph Day, and for naming your second son after him. It proves you had a bigger soul than him or his brutal overseers. He had three thousand acres and eighty slaves near Marshallville, Georgia. I'm not proud of this. You said Judge Day was a good man. Yes, he was good to you alright. He gave each slave family a shack and garden with a plot for tobacco. Why, he even let them raise and sell chickens, make blackberry wine and persimmon beer. What's more, the good Judge never sold a slave. He let families stay intact. Yet the Judge's wife thought he spoiled them. Oh, how he spoiled them by making his slaves pick cotton six days a week, stooping from dawn to dusk dragging seventy-pound sacks. Those with weak backs crawled along the rows on their knees. They plucked cotton balls from sharp bolls until their fingers bled.

Meanwhile, at meals in the big house, slave boys waved peacock feathers over the food to brush the flies away. You say the Judge never had a dispute and whipped no one. That's right—he just let his overseers do the dirty work. No wonder people tried to escape, smearing turpentine on the soles of their feet to throw off the scent. You say he looked like a Christian, but as the Georgia Speaker of the House, Judge Day made and enforced slave laws for twenty-five years. No black person slave or free was allowed to read or write, to own a house, or travel without a pass. Even slaveholders couldn't free a slave without the legislature's permission. He had the power to do good, but this good Christian man did none. There was no good slave-owner—no more than a good pedophile or a good guard at Auschwitz. Instead, he carved slave laws on the backs of those in bondage—whiplash scars made with pen and ink. Racism, the great eraser, rubs out everyone's humanity. Maybe deep down, he felt like a motherless child . . .

My great-grandaunt once saw an old slave crush tobacco in his palm then stuff the shreds in his pipe and light it with a burning coal taken from the hearth with his fingers. Like the coal that seared the prophet's lips, to crush racism we must pick up the cinders of truth and justice with our bare hands and carry the fire together. I regret these words won't reach you or your parents, George and Emily, and all the people the Judge owned. But I promise you, I won't let the fire go out. Not ever.

FOOTWASH BAPTISTS OF BOYLE COUNTY

(For Pastor Betty Clark)

We never had no fancy home,
just a prefab kit house mailed
from Sears and Roebuck. Walls
threadbare as an empty promise.
No electricity. We peed in the dark.
Water pumped from the well flushed
when you sat on the throne. At five,
I feared I'd be washed away.

We sharecropped tobacco,
primed the leaves by hand,
and hoicked them high
under tin roofs. They hung down
to cure like long brown ears
of Daddy's hounds.

We never knew what poor was—
we always had new shoes each year
and plenty of collards, rabbits, and squirrels.
Sometimes, we stole chickens.
I wept when my pet pig Suzie
became dinner. We fed on joy singing
with Daddy's guitar and drank up tunes
that poured from our beat-up radio.

Sundays, I'd put on my best dress
and we'd walk down the holler
to the Footwash Baptist Church.
Everyone washed everyone's feet.
It gave us a chance to be like Jesus,
to be treated like kings and queens
sitting up high in our white robes,
like having our shoes shined
but without shoes.

I WOKE TO HEAR A RAVEN SING

She croaked her Gaelic song
in the tar-black night
and slit the skin of sky,

making the thermal stars shrink
with terror—afraid they too
would be gutted by this gastric sound,

by the shriek that killed all sense
of hope, of safety and self—
the spastic cry of Medea
mourning for her children.

Awake and shivering,
I stood barefoot and alone
in the moon-swollen light
staring out my stark window

wondering if death
had learned
to sing.

OWL, FISHING AT NIGHT

Once, when clouds were heavy
and gray, it swooped down secretly
like a dark, curious angel,
perched beneath a canopy of green
and stared at us inside
with amber eyes.

Often I hear it in the pines
behind the house hooting
its message long after night
has flung her bolt of black lamé.
Last night, it yanked me
from my barge of sleep, clutching
my dream in its claws like a fish.

I never know to feel sad
or soothed when I hear
its three hollow calls
thinking it will soon
find a home
in some other wood.

So I listen
and let its wooden bowl
of sound rock me,
rock me to sleep,
hoping it will fish
for my dreams and stay
one more night.

THE LATHE OF JOY

She thrusts her sword
into the niche of my heart
reserved for beauty,
and with her glittering
and polished awl
shapes it to hold more.

Then she flies to her perch,
a hummingbird in a tree,
and wipes her long beak
back and forth on a twig—
a tiny fencer sharpening
her foil of quick lightning.

When she is gone,
I languish, hoping
to hear the bright burr
of her wings whirling
once more near the wheel
of my incessant desire.

SNOWY OWL

It hears a heartbeat hiding
under the snow.

With 3D ears, the hunter tracks
the course, distance, and height

of the faint thrum which digs down
thinking, like us, it has outwitted death.

The white head swivels
like a lighthouse beacon

and rising in air on the beat of wings
dives like a cold glass spear

then flies blithely away, its claws
gripping whatever the snow once held,

and leaves a white imprint of wings.
And I thought, maybe death

is like God, able to hear
what moves in our depths,

what cries to be uttered,
and longing to free us

from the deep cold sleep,
carries us away.

ARRIBADA: THE OLIVE RIDLEY SEA TURTLES ARRIVE

When the wind, tide and moon are right,
they arrive, pushed by the barrel-thrust
of the sea. Lumbering from the shore

they come, hundreds of thousands
or more, like legions of helmets
storming the beach at Normandy.

Laden with galaxies of eggs, they take
their journey slow. Each one knows
where they have to go. They carve

a furrow in the sand, crawling
with flippered fins until they reach a spot
then dig and drop their string of pearls.

They carefully sweep the sand
as vultures stalk the beach, then turn,
sluggish as ships, and head back to sea.

They know where they're meant to be.

In the fullness of time, small bald heads
poke like Samurai from the sand.
They rush en masse to the shore

to beat the greedy beaks and O!
death's dark unsparing wings.
The sea's magnetic whoosh

tells them where to go.

NIGHT OF TWO MOONS

"Enlightenment is like the moon reflected on the water.
The moon does not get wet, nor is the water broken."
—Dogen

I rise long before dawn and pad in my bare feet
and bathrobe to get a glass of water. Out

my south bedroom window I can see
a full orange moon, not the plump harvest moon

that smiles and waves hello every fall,
but a sickly ocher moon floating in a smoky sky,

as if the man in the moon had spent too much time
in a tanning bed. In the kitchen, I look

out the window facing north
and see another moon hiding

behind a twisted matrix of trees
where I know the moon shouldn't be.

Turns out the puzzling moon
is but a reflection in my neighbor's window.

How like this odd year 2020,
four digits with two moons, like the word

moon itself, its O's like two moons colliding.
2020, the year of the fake moon and the real.

And I remember the famous koan about the moon
and the water, how the wide moon is reflected

in one drop of dew on the grass. Not two but many moons.
Then it hits me, like a stone tossed into a pool.

You fool, I scold myself, for thinking the mirror was real.
When will the water ever be unbroken?

II

THE BELL RINGERS OF BREDWARDINE

John, the bell master, stood still
in a circle of five, each one holding
at handstroke his candy cane sally.
Then he called, "Look to! Treble's going. She's gone,"
and yanked his rope down. Four
quickly followed, driving their ropes
into the ground as the sound
of Grandsire Doubles tumbled
from five metal bells, each note
a silver ball bouncing off the walls
of the old stone tower.

They were pile drivers, arms
rising up and down—each body
throbbing with swing and sound
of bells and metal tongues
dancing and pulsing in the belfry.

Sometimes, John called the changes:
single, bob, round, or *stand*
as the five switched, clicking into gear
without a hitch. For two hours, peals
cascaded down as the red-faced ringers
sweated like long-distance runners,
stinking up the room like a gym.
As they rang, I strolled out from the church
to gaze as autumn pinned a full moon
like a pearl brooch to the blue-black sky,
amazed at my marvelous luck.

Later, over beer at the Red Lion Inn
Diana tells me she's not musical
but with a bell her one note is a song.
"When I ring, we make music together,
and I go home feeling alive."

The ringers ended by ringing
down the bells, going from one to five
with shorter and shorter pulls
but faster and faster peals
until the whole tower hummed
with harmonics of ecstatic sound
and the bell master said, "Stand!"

Five bells stopped at once,
and the whole ringing valley stood still.

OUR LADY BURNING, APRIL 2019

Notre Dame, that grand old lady getting a face-lift,
looked like a dowager crowned with a hairnet of steel.

Then fire, smoke! Flames engulfed the spire first
like a burning finger pointing to God,

and spread to the hidden forest of beams.
Stained-glass saints wept red-blue tears,

embers rained fiery hail as if Mary's
sacred heart was burning out of control.

When the roof caved in,
the stones stopped singing.

Outside, people watched in shock and terror
as flames staunched the fountainhead.

They wept, knelt in prayer, sang hymns.
Strangers hugged and consoled each other,

tasting grief's caustic ash, breathing ungodly air.
That Holy Week, Paris, and indeed the whole world,

prayed with one voice, one heart,
on ancient cobbled streets,

right there in an open-air cathedral shared
by us all, with its vaulting blue roof

that touches fiery suns
but never burns.

DEAD LETTER DROP

"I find letters from God dropped in the street
and every one is signed . . . "
—Walt Whitman, "Song of Myself," *Leaves of Grass*

God writes so seldom now, I think
he uses lemon juice for ink.

His notes are coded ciphers hid in hollow rocks.
I'm lucky if I can find one in St. James Park.

I've given up on God's game of hide and seek,
much less deciphering his sideways scrawl.

Did he stop writing for a reason?
We never had a fight or falling out.

Or did we stop talking, like an old couple
of fifty years eating their meals in silence?

What of those letters from our first love affair?
The prayers so hot, each one immolated itself?

Each one bleeding with longing and desire
and a devouring need to disappear into the other.

Doesn't that count for something?
Or were those prayers just seeds

meant to be buried then die in the ground
so an invisible tree could take root

each branch bearing green leaves that flame
with their own words of love before they die?

BEGGAR'S FEAST

Inside you, need sits eager
and alone like a blind beggar
squatting at the busy intersection
of your heart hoping to hear
the gold coin of communion
clanging in the bottom
of her tin cup.

You never see it coming
when someone drops
this coin, sudden
and unearned,
into the altar
of your hand.

You'll know it by the way
the old roadblocks of fear
and grief are lifted,
when your body for once
breathes deeply—
when even a fallen crumb
tastes like a golden feast.

SAYING MASS WITH ANGELS

The usual crowd gathers round the altar:
grannies, young mothers, babies bundled
in slings like marsupials. A boy

with blonde curls plays quietly, heedless,
as the tracery of high Tudor prose
glides off my tongue.

He rolls his plastic car back
and forth on the altar rail, absorbed
by his toy's private journey.

But when I say, "With Angels and Archangels,
and with all the company of heaven,"
he stops and looks up,

frightened, I suspect, by the thought
of a real angel floating down
from our wooden vaulting.

(Seeing faith and fear mingled in his small,
stunned face makes me weak-kneed—
a spotless mirror of palpable Spirit.)

But what if a real angel had drifted down
which only he could see, her ethereal gown
billowing in the air? What if she knelt by him,

her merry eyes softening with love,
and nudged his car along the rail
just to see him smile and resume his play?

WHEN A SAINT GROWS OLD

(In Memory of Fr. James Thompson Brown: 1927-2019)

Each day came to him as gift:
the fruited vine, the braided wheat,
the winking stars—each
a stepping stone to God.

He always held an inner radiance
like a man born to be a lamp.
When he spoke, he bounced
on the balls of his feet—
but at ninety, joy buoyed him up
as if he danced on clouds.

Even when words slipped
from the prompter's box buried
under the floorboards of his brain,
he shone brighter still. I think his loss
of words lifted the last roadblock
between him and God.

Once he stopped and stood
with his hand on a tree trunk
as if to catch his breath, but stayed
for the longest time. Soon
it was clear he had moved

to a place beyond words—fluent
in the diction of rising sap, chanting
the psalms of dappled leaves,
feeling the greening spark
charged from earth's deepest core.

When the window is filled
with light,
the glass disappears.

THE JONAH COMPLEX

"Have you had sight of me, Jonas, My child? Mercy within mercy within mercy . . . I looked upon what was nothing. I touched what was without substance, and within what was not, I am."
—Thomas Merton, *The Sign of Jonas*

Larger than galaxies is the triple mercy.
Its relentless weight bears down like a vice.

It clamps upon you above and below.
It mounts from within like liquid fire.

You try to explain but no one understands.
You flee. You go west to escape but can't.

It follows you wherever you go. There is no place
to hide. All your exits are arrivals. You sink

beneath the uprush and backwash of the sea.
Ribbons of kelp strangle you. Immense things

engulf you. Death spits you out like sputum
from its mouth. You land as flotsam on the shore of yes.

This is heaven's intent—to squeeze all the darkness
out of you until you're fused into a diamond.

CAPEL-Y-FFIN

(In Memory of Ruth Bidgood: 1922-2022)

1

Once Kilvert, the heart-thwarted diarist,
climbed from Hay up the rugged track
of Gospel Pass to the church nesting
by seven dark yews. Critical
or curious, maybe both, he came
to see this haunted place and quiz
the new-made monks in black.

In the heyday of summer, the year
after Kilvert died, before twilight's
footfall hushed their game, choir boys
played below the cloister grange,
laughing freely in the high green field.
One boy waiting to run felt a wisp
of wind finger his hair—turning
he saw a blazing light above the hedge.

What he saw was a woman, her hands
raised in prayer. She glided toward him,
a phosphorescence edged in gold.
He stared, not with fear but awe, as she drifted
so close he could see the folds
of her robe. He longed to touch her, be
with her always, but she melted like dew

into a bush of wild rhubarb, brushing
its broad leaves as she left. A glow
like fire-flung smoke followed behind.

The other boys saw her too
and ran to the abbey panting with joy,
"We saw her in the field, the Lady
all golden and glorious!"
They were not believed,
but lectured sternly, and tested.
But later visions confirmed the first.

The monk said, "The last
circle of light flashed in the sky
so large, it embraced the Chapel,
mountains and trees. Everything.
Light, pulsing like a heart,
splashed upon our feet.
It consumed the Black Hills
as if the Vale of Ewyas
were lifted heaven high."

2

Like Kilvert before me,
I came to see the abbey
and its cockeyed chapel,
tower-tilted, "squatting,"
he said, "like a stout gray owl."

I was simply glad to be
where Kilvert had walked,
to see the twisted yews
and step among the tipsy graves—
the slabs all splotched with lichen
and moss. I saw no vision, heard

no ancient song. I was glad to be
where the sun once fell,
where long ago, holy leaves
of rhubarb healed the wounds
of a doubting nun—yet yearned to feel
the light's full-fall from that same sun.

ODE TO VELÁZQUEZ'S DWARF
AND OTHERS

Let's hear it for history's little people.
Consider Sebastián de Morra, dwarf
and court jester to King Phillip IV of Spain.

I met him as I flipped through a book of art
from the Prado Museum, a short man
with eyes fierce as Antonio Banderas's

and dressed in orange satin and lace.
He sits with his fists on his thighs as if to say,
"So, what's your beef?"

Dwarfs in King Philip's court were treated like pets,
like oracles. They could say anything and did.
(At any size, it takes guts to speak truth to power.)

Small people never had it easy. Sir Jeffry Hudson was eight
when he met King Charles I after being encased in a pie
and later, was nabbed by Barbary pirates but, who knows how,
escaped.

Others, like Tom Thumb, found fame in the circus,
and MGM made munchkins immortal. But most impressive
is St. Neot, half-brother of King Alfred the Great.

A priest, scholar, and hermit, he was so holy,
they said a key in the door bent down to meet his hand.
When thieves stole his ox, he used a deer to plow his field.

85

Seeing this, the thieves repented and returned the ox. He forgave
and blessed them. And so they became monks and he their abbot.
St. Neot even cured King Alfred of a famous case of piles,

then inspired him to defeat the Danes. So you see,
without little people there'd be no England, no America.
Who knew our debt to them would be so tall?

A VISITATION

Who knows how long,
    from your unripe birth until now,
        the unknown guide waited
            for the right time to speak.

The words are petals,
    floating in wind, lifted
        from a place unknown, landing

like a half-remembered dream
    whose light breaks in
        and stops you on the sidewalk.

The playground disappears,
    and the corner house.
        Birds halt in mid-air,

sounds muffle, as someone
    stands beside you
        in an aureole charged

with bright atoms
    or condensed stars that close
        the place between spaces,

    and takes your hand.

In a flash of knowing—
    just as you know this hand
        has held yours since the day

you were born with all its trauma
    and unfolding risk—
        the words ring in your mind

like the ting of crystal,
    "I have to go now."

You spend the rest of your life
    puzzled by time's
        translucent cracks

once lit by voice and touch,
    always reaching, reaching
        for a hand

withdrawn.

IN A DARK WOOD

I walk down an old, narrow road,
cracked macadam, rarely traveled.
I don't know where it ends.
Here's a place where somebody
fell off a cliff and died. A shrine
marks the spot: candles, stones,
a beer bottle. The Virgin of Guadalupe
bends over red plastic roses.

I don't know where I'm going,
but I go on, stopping at a wooden gate
plush with lichen and green moss.
The path below disappears
into a thicket, smothered
by the forest's luxuriance.
Even now, I could turn back—
but don't.

With a click of the latch,
I'm in a primordial world,
silent, birdless, a few ferns,
but no flowers. My feet
spring on soft pine duff.
I press through briars, crawl
over felled trunks and staunch rocks
until I reach the grandfather tree.

It is so tall,
the fretwork of branches
sweeps the scattered clouds.

At the base, the core is hollow—
wider than my arm-span.
I step through the threshold
into a charred cathedral,
a high black vault
carved by living flames.

Inside this scorched cave,
I close my eyes,
hear nothing.
The faint lick
of flame burns within.

LINES INSPIRED BY BACH'S LAST FUGUE

Music as the art of stillness
collecting itself into presence.
A consortium of melody
drawing a fluid bead of intelligence
down the mind's windowpane.
The hollow call of wood doves
hidden among the pines.
The Arch-Lute of your soul.
The Untouchable, yet touching.
The unspoken question, always seeking
the same answer: "What is death
but the still point between breaths
we breathe daily—only more?"
The lyric of your life.
The ceaseless duet
between faith and doubt
until it stops.

WHAT DREAMS MAY COME

Upstairs I am looking out a French double window
where green ivy hugs the brick wall.
There's my family, my friend Roussel
and, of all people, Mark Twain
with his thicket of hair, drooping mustache,
and white crumpled suit.
They lounge in the garden below.
I open the dormer,
"Hi everyone, I'm here!"
They look up, then poof—
they're gone. I'm alone

shut out of the dream,
standing in a padded cell.
No way out. I pound the walls
and shout, trying to re-enter
the old dream. Suddenly,
the floor opens and I'm freefalling
into darkness, clawing the air
hoping to grab a branch,
a trapeze, anything to hang onto,
praying I won't hit bottom.
There is no bottom, just eternal space.

I jerk awake,
afraid to sleep again,
alone with the afterthought,
is this what death is like?
Waiting for the sweet light of dawn,
I lie in bed, thankful
for many things
but worry (don't we all?)
where the next dream
will take me.

COMPLINE, GETHSEMANI ABBEY, 1973

Like Jesus, I have to go through Nazareth
to get there. I drive hell-bent
to reach the church in time,
but lose my way.

As dusk throws its purple shawl
over the Kentucky knobs, hushing
the sizzle of cicadas, I arrive late, frazzled—
my pilgrimage wrecked.

Cursing myself for missing worship,
I race to the gallery where below, song flows
from a hundred white-robed monks—
each man a cathedral of prayer.

As they chant to Mary's icon,
beeswax flames lick the dark
and my eyes widen. Her gold leaf shines.
Their song invokes the Presence.

It broods around us thicker than honey,
lighter than light. No choice but to fall
on my knees. My soul rises as if filled
with helium and someone released the string.

THE TOUCHSTONE

Redwoods Monastery, 2019

When Thomas Merton was here,
he photographed giant logs, cross-crossed
and tumble-tossed like pick-up sticks—
trunks of redwood trees that long since
had sloughed off their shaggy hides.

Fifty years on, I have come to stand
before one last log, last remnant
of the pile, long after Merton was felled
far too soon. Its bulk shines like chrome

in the noonday sun. I touch its side, hard
as the gray body of a beached whale
that once carried Merton (another Jonah),
to this place, just as his words carry me.

I touch it to feel where his hand touched.
He teaches me to be human when some days
I fail to remember it. I love how his hands
planted pines and Zen stone gardens,

and found true wilderness
in a cabin. His hand that pushed a pen
when it least wanted to move, like my hand
when the mind's inkwell dries.

Fed on raven's bread, he tossed living words
to a famished world, filled with the burden
and promise of possibility. Words that even now
guide me to walk across stars and water.

THE LURE FROM A DISTANT ROOM

"By ceasing to question the sun, I have become light."
—Thomas Merton, from "O Sweet Irrational Worship"

It was not when he poked his finger
into that red-lanced wound
and flipped the flap of skin
that he found faith—no,
it was when he dared to cross
the line of reason, touching
the edge of shipwreck,
into that upper room.

Born skeptic, he always wore his doubt
as armor, as a badge of honor.
For days he mocked the morbid tales
that made the women shout for joy.
He knew better than to believe
a pipe dream. Even Peter,
ever practical, fell for it,
the bit about Jesus being real
and not a ghost—tangible
as bread.

Once, he would have died
for Him, but Golgotha proved
he was foolish to follow his heart.

You bet he wasn't going to make
that mistake again.

Yet something kept pushing
despite the questions and qualms,
luring him like music from a distant room.
Was it curiosity? Or something deeper—
the hot ember of irrational need
searing inside him?
It was a miracle he came at all,
as the burly guards of hope
and love thrust him up the stairs
(despite his old Adversary
shouting in his brain.)

At the door, dropping
his chains of fear,
breaking logic's grip,
he knocked.

WIDOW'S MITE

Like tossing cargo
from a sinking ship
she dropped two

copper coins, worth
a day's wage,
(her soul's one extravagance)
into the box

then went home to eat
her last pittance of meal,
not knowing what Jesus saw
or said, not knowing

thousands of years later,
the clink of her coins
can still be heard.

PIETÀ

The mother from Buzkova
knelt by his feet, not draped
like Mary, all in blue,
but wearing a brown hooded sweatshirt.

Is it nothing to you,

His body looked like he had dived
into the manhole head first.
Only his shoes showed.

all you who pass by?

When she recognized them,
she shrieked and wailed,
bending double with grief.

Look and see

When the men pulled his body out
and wrapped it, not in linen,
but white plastic, she cried,
"Let me see him! My son!
Yevhennii, Yevhennii!"

if there is any sorrow

Yevhennii, whose name
means "well-born."

like my sorrow.

"Let me look, let me look!"
But the men kept her from him.

THE REAL WORK

(For the Rev. Zoila Schoenbrun)

"What kind of parents are they?"
she asked her friends staring down
at me in their tennis whites.
Only four, a free-range kid,
I sat howling with panic and fear
as my bare feet bled from shards
of broken glass and my life
poured out on the playground sand.
They mopped me up with tissues
and Band-Aids, then I limped
two blocks home for lunch.

It took me years to find
the gentle hand that healed
my injured life. You, the priest
with soft voice and kind eyes,
led the way and named
the wounds, adept as the blind
at reading dashes and welts
raised on a page.

Yet an unseen deeper hand has done
most of the work—forming me
from the inside, molding me
into my true shape, teaching me
my soul's work: to shed my shoes,
walk barefoot on forgiving ground.

HOW TRUE POEMS BEGIN

Before they become words, poems
twirl like a hot push of wind
rustling up an echo
in the gray canyons of the mind.

There are always two poems
within a poem: words that haunt you,
hanging their musk of meaning
in midair like verbal gardenias,

and the sudden sputtering of thought
that combusts into words,
reactive as photons flashing
their surprised sparklers.

True poems nest in the calm
between words—each space
a soft sirocco
breathing us and the poems
into being.

WHEN I'M AN OLD WOMAN

(For Dr. Roussel Sargent on her 90th Birthday)
(After Jenny Joseph)

When I'm an old woman, I'll forget
about purple and red garish hats,
and spend all my money on charities
and chocolate. I'll lavish my care
on two fractious cats—one fat,
one black with four white spats.
I'll sport a cane and thwack
careless cars that cross my path,
collect English calendars, hoard
calfskin books, and save
copper pennies in a jar. I'll buy
Christmas crackers and wear paper hats
to make up for the gravity of my youth.
I'll go to the Sussex Downs to gaze
at orient wheat, then dip my toes
in icy brooks and dream of Greece.
I'll feast on steak and Stilton,
drink the finest port, and lounge
by yellow beeches in the fall.

At all times and in all places,
I will cherish words, never miss Jeopardy,
and let the sound of Tudor prose
lift my soul. I'll bask in evensong
as tower bells sing their silver scales
then stay up till two digging through the OED,

sleep in late, and dawdle over coffee
and the crosswords. I'll write
witty notes to Ben Zimmer full
of questions about words like zounds,
boogie, and flabbergaster then read
the *Times Literary Supplement*
from cover to cover and tell my friends
never, under any circumstance,
to vote for the GOP.

When Death comes north of ninety,
civil as Emily's coachman,
he'll hand me saffron roses
then open the door
to my bright future—my life
as a living poem,
a golden word,
everlasting in the poetry of Christ.

QUIRKY PAINTINGS OF CHRIST'S ASCENSION

Hans Süss von Kulmbach's *Ascension*
makes me laugh. Two feet hang down
like pale chandeliers just below the top
of the frame over the heads of Mary
Christ's mother and the twelve apostles
(or eleven men with Magdalene hiding
in the crowd), all adoring, not God
or Jesus ascending, but two punctured duck-feet.

Maybe Hans ran out of room
or he'd have imagined Jesus
rising in glory, like a future
Franky Zapata lifting above
the Champs Elysees jet-propelled
on his hover board, waving
goodbye in benediction
on his way to his heavenly throne.

More mind-bending is Dali's *Ascension*.
Two large soles of Christ's feet,
now healed, float close to the viewer.
Christ rises (arms outstretched,
his hands contorted, frozen in agony),
toward the head of a giant sunflower,
the golden nucleus of life, to join
Spirit-dove and God the Mother.

Dali places the viewer right where
the apostles stood, beneath
the feet of Christ as he floats above
and beyond. Whenever I see this,
I can barely stand—but I wonder

what was it like to watch him leave
(for the second time) as he rose?
After he was gone, when in grief
they looked down, did they see
his footprints in the dust?

LOVE'S NECESSITY

To be the within, within the way
where in us there was no room;
To be the room within the home
where all can come and stay;
To say the unsaid for all the unseen;
To be the true bread for all the unclean;
To die a slow death and not presume to say
whose hand shall ply the killing steel;
This then is Love—who pours out His breath
and gives to us friends
His very last meal.

ST. FRANCIS XAVIER MISSION

Kahnawake, Quebec, Canada, 2019

St. Kateri, drunk with Christ's love,
groped half-blind two hundred miles
on foot through blowdown and scrub,
past the mighty Cloudsplitter
to become his bride in this place.

Like her, I have come thousands
of miles to reach the red doors
of this holy house that stands
stalk still in our modern wasteland
as a common crane.

I too grope with foggy faith,
hoping to feel the feather
of grace lift me higher. I sit
by her tomb, a long block
white as the milk of crushed lilies,

and I wait. Beeswax candles
pour their honey cense into the air.
Soon, a palpable cloak of softness
wraps around me—a velvet cave
I don't want to leave.

It's as if her prayers from ages past
keep transmitting through the air,
searching for a thirsting heart,
a wavelength open and tuned
enough to receive them.

SABBATH SOIL

(For the Rev. Gayle Pershouse Vaughn: 1943-2020)

Drop me, O God, like a plumb stone
down your great in-delving deep,
from rim to sinking fathom
down the darkening well
of your bottomless heart.
I do not fear my freefall into fallowness.

This is no dusty ditch of defeat—
but rather the full swell
of emptiness, the need of fusty roots
digging down. Tapping bedrock
in the dark, I sift the essence
of your Sabbath soil.

PRAYER

(After George Herbert)

Christ's welcome feast, purest bread,
Music at midnight, torched tongues,
Dark lightning, hope for the dead,
A whisper barely heard, Sabbath rest,
Words that embrace, Spirit's gold,
Hands that mend, battered clouds,
Grace for the worst and best,
Doubter's ditch, a desperate leap,
Lifeboat for sinners, God's lure,
Key to Christ's heart, a murmured psalm,
Sword of God's Word, a mountain steep,
Saints' recreation, highest mirth,
Love's kindest knot, the soul's food,
Dove's firefall, the Vine's precious blood.

WHAT BODY?

For some people, the body
is a Coney Island, made for cheap thrills.
For others, it's a cash cow or a cart
to carry their brain around.

My quirk is to lean toward the soul,
not five senses but the sixth sense—
the spirit's messenger, a white
red-eyed, red-clawed dove.

St. Francis said his body was a cell—
not a prison but a private hermitage.
I believe this until I get a hangnail
or have a root canal or break a bone.

Then the body becomes a two-bit dictator,
shouting and banging his fist,
insisting things return
to the way they were.

Maybe our bodies are more like the sky
obscured by canopies of clouds
veiling depths and weather.
Made from the dust of stars,

we are galaxies full of gifts,
stories, and dreams—
living heirlooms we pass along
before we die.

My days slip away
like minnows I can't catch.
Once, I fit inside a shoebox;
one day, I'll need something bigger.

Maybe, when it's about over,
I'll be more attached to my body,
sweet temple
where the white dove lives.

MASSAGE SESSION

Lying face down, my forehead
cradled by a soft horseshoe,
I drift with the melody of a flute
as sandalwood musk cloys the air.
Her hands, greased with almond oil,
knead my arms, legs, the slope of my back
like bread. Her thumbs climb the ladder of fire,
pressing poisonous stress from my spine.

After I dress, she tells me that the room
was crammed just now with the dead
I once helped in hospice. Skeptical
of mediums but curious, "How many?"
I ask. "More than a hundred," she says.
"Standing room only. They came
to thank you for your care."

I picture hundreds of ghosts
standing in the room, looking
at me naked with nothing
but a towel draped over my rear.
Not the best time for a reunion.

How did so many fit inside one room?
Were some at the edge cut in half
by the wall? Did they look the same
as before? Or did they youthen in heaven—
their faces like those in wedding and prom
photos propped up on tripods at their funerals?

I forget most of their names but remember the ones
I loved best: Leslie who adored Amish quilts,
Belva who occupied Alcatraz, Gayle a Choctaw twin,
Harold whose father bootlegged, Mavis, so English
and gracious, Henry the scientist-priest, and Dick
the deacon who knew the Railway Key System by heart.

I'm not sure what to do next in case some
are still there. I pause and consider
my options, then address the empty air,
"You're welcome. I was honored to help."
I figure it doesn't pay to annoy a ghost
in this life or the next.

III

TREADING ON HOLY GROUND:
HOSPICE POEMS

1.

DEATH IS A TERRIBLE MENTOR

Death smokes a cigarette
and taps on Twitter by the pool
as you sink for the third time.
He puts up his feet and has a highball
as you're having a heart attack.
He leaves guns lying around the house
for kids and misfits to find.
He forgets to fix the brakes,
the gas stove, the rickety stairs.
He buys you drugs, booze, or pills
saying one more won't hurt.
He lets tumors burrow
inside your bowels, clots blow
like balloons in your brain.
He shakes your hand and sails
your cruise ship to the River Styx.

Then, just when you think you've beat him,
death bustles into your house,
a night nurse with armloads of diapers.
He moves your bed into the parlor,
sits up all hours until you fall
into your final sleep, then slips
a silver coin on the night stand
and leaves it for others
to clean up the mess.

Death has nothing to do
with the health department and cares
even less about teaching. You'd think
he'd hang flyers on your doorknob
with black-box warnings or advice
on how to get more out of life,
start a class called Death and Dying 101.
But no, death is a terrible mentor—

but by God you learn.

2.

AT THE VILLA

In suburbia, they aren't called rest homes anymore.
Upscale and spotless, silk bouquets
grace the concierge desk and all the tables
down the hall. And let's not forget the marble foyers,
the crystal doors, the Laura Ashley prints
with matching wallpaper, the salmon rugs,
microwaves, and latest gadgets
nobody knows how to work.

Sure, a few concessions are made to old Methuselah,
as if he were an arthritic lawyer from Memphis
wearing black suspenders and a wrinkled shirt.
But you can bet everyone pays
for the handrails and the bathroom grips,
the call bells for aides who never come,
the nurses, the cooks, the dieticians, and drivers,
and of course, the activities director.

Ray tells me this is no place to live.
Life here was born stale.
Back home, things were messy,
but at least you knew your neighbors—
like Mrs. Swenson, who at ninety
still canned her own pears. At home
there was always something to do:
mend a gate, shell peas, chop wood,

sit on the porch, or shoot the breeze
with friends passing by. Even
the good earth beneath your feet
was yours to plant and hoe.
Your ripe tomatoes tasted sweeter
because they grew by your own hands.

"Here," Ray says, "you only get plastic pots
to grow things in. The sun shines strong
in just one place, too far for me to walk."
Once, he tried planting tomatoes.
They grew,
but someone swiped them.

"It's like they think we forgot
how to be human," he says,
looking down. And I
a chaplain here
but for an hour,
take his hand.

3.

THE LATECOMER

He put on a robe and slowly
stretched his body onto the couch.
The coffee table was strewn
with the detritus of disease: a phone,
pills, lotion, Kleenex, straws,
and half-drunk bottles of Ensure.
Unshaved and pale, he smelled
of damp sheets.

To answer my question,
he said, "I was seventy-nine
when the doctor told me
straight out, 'You got cancer.'
Well, that sure jerked the wheels
off my wagon.

"So, first thing I thought was,
'you better get right with the Lord.'
See, I got saved when I was sixteen,
but I stopped going to church
because all the boys called me sissy.
Of course, I regret it now.

"I went to my church Elder brother
and asked if God would take me back.
'Sure,' he said, 'God takes latecomers
just like anyone else.'

"When they put me in the water,
I felt like I was a throwback,
a fish too short to keep.
It makes you kind of small
to come up next to God.
He covers a lot of territory."

When he was done, he covered
his eyes with his arm to hide
the light. Seeing his words
weighed heavy, I prayed silently
then rose, closed the door,
and left him to sleep.

4.

THE ZEN OF DYING

You perch on your bed,
snared by snaking tubes.
Lipstick and blush, left
untouched on your bureau,
are relics from your old life.
Puffy as a pillow,
you're a pale Buddha.

Finding the cell phone
is your primary mission.
Next it's clamping the tubes,
taking the pills, having a pee,
and, yes, more ice chips please.

The slide show of your life
slips by—a montage
of your greatest hits.
You love family photos best—
sacred stills of the heart.

You step into rooms
where no one else can go.
Rooms where redbirds fly,
and blonde boys
(two lost sons) pass invisibly.

You say, "There's no such thing
as wasted time." You know
wasted time is better
than no time at all.

For you, each moment
melts away like drops
of butterscotch.
The Dharma says
the secret to dying
lies in letting go.

Soon you will forget
even how to grasp.

5.

GOD'S SLOW ANSWER

Once trim, bronzed and svelte,
a knock-out in a bikini,
you're now the target of rebels,
a deadly army of cells,
a molecular coup d'état.

Moonfaced, you avoid mirrors,
dreading to see your body
swollen as a blowfish.
Your bones pour out like milk.
Hoarse cries of your heart
rise up. Your mouth
is awash with ash. Like Job,
your prayers pummel deaf ears,
demanding answers.

Your goal is to stand
in your own kitchen,
to command your body again.
To reclaim your life.
Small victories come
in mastering small tasks:
walking without help
across the room,
making scrambled eggs,
steeping a cup of tea.

But God's slow answer
comes
one heartbreaking day
at a time.

6.

ALL I CAN DO

Your hand clings to your crystal rosary
that glitters like a string of teardrops
and even though you cross yourself
when you take your drugs,
pain's sword skewers
your brittle bones. Your body
throbs with pain poured
out like hot gold from a smelter.

I wince as you thrust your hand
erect in the air—pleading
to death, God, or anyone
to end the torture. I am
a stranger sitting close by,
witness to pain I cannot douse.

I come not as a healer
just a priest with no means
to stop the knife that guts you
like a fish, can only sit mute
beside you and hold your hand
as Spanish prayers rise
from your cracked lips, whispering
with tongues of parched leaves,
the lament of a weeping guitar.

7.

MORTAL SHAME

It's the suspense
that kills you. *What am I*
supposed to do—just lie here
and wait until I die?

At two in the morning,
you can hear each grain
of sand in time's hourglass
drop, drop, drop.

Daylight never comes soon enough.

When death finally arrives,
surprisingly courteous
at the old chop block,
it's a relief. The ax
weighs heavy in his hands.

Needing control, some prefer
to do their own dirty work:
pills, hanging, a gun.
They depart without bending
the knee or forgiving—
even themselves.

Some never leave a note
or make time to say goodbye.
I don't want them
to see me this way.

Like they're ashamed
of being mortal.

8.

LOST

Hunched in her wheelchair,
she turns to me and raises
the twigs of her fingers:

You have to help me!

How can I help you?

You have to get me out of here—
you have to take me home!"

And where is home?

Home?! Home?! That's the problem,
nobody knows where home is.
Nobody knows! Nobody understands!

She stares fiercely at the thin soup
set before her, lifts the bowl
to her mouth with two hands
and gulps it to the dregs
as if hemlock.

9.

I THOUGHT IT WAS A TOILET

No, it's a wastepaper basket.

This is such a nuisance!

What is?

When I look up.

What do you see?

Nothing. . . But I remember.

What do you remember?

New York.

How was it?

It's not normal.   How long do I have to stay here?

Do you want to go back to bed?

Yes. That's my walker. Is this the way to my room?

Yes, that's the way.

I can't find it.

What can't you find?

I'm looking for me.

10.

FLOATING NOWHERE FAST

Bedbound, moored
to his mattress,
he's a landlocked ship.
He measures his days
by the length of shadows,
drifts on morphine clouds,
floating farther away
from himself day by day.

Archie Bunker reruns flicker
on the TV he never sees.
He says the noise keeps him
from feeling lonely. His cancer
has made him bald as a stone.
He slurs, *The worst part of dying,*
is having to put up with Bruce Willis jokes.

Spirits of friends and family hover
by his bed. At night, strangers
appear at his bedroom door. Finally,
his sister Mary, who died of MS,
comes saying it is time to go.
He tells me: *She stands upright now*
and says she walks everywhere.
Me, I'm done with walking;
I want to go home in a car.

11.

SWIMMING LESSON

This is how it works. When a child,
they took you out to Myrtle Beach
where the undertow dragged you
to the bottom of the world.
But you didn't drown. So,
you never learned to swim.

Now, everything grows dark.
You sit trembling at the edge
of blazing water. Your lover
has already jumped in and,
from far out at sea,
is waving (not drowning.)
He calls, "Come on in,
the water's fine!"

You want nothing more
than to be with him—
but you never learned to swim.
The door to the world
is shutting fast behind you.
So you let out the deepest sigh,
and say, "OK, I give up."

And with one stroke,
you jump.

12.

DYING TIME

You can see those invisible visitors
    crowding round your bed,
can feel their thickened presence
    like mist fogging your bathroom mirror.

They press against the slender membrane
    between this world and the next.
It quivers—a silver moon-trail
    rippling in the dark.

Then with one last tremor,
    as darkness spills into day
morning brings its blessing,
    you leave your shell and step
over time's liquid line.

They say in death one is the same
    as they ever were, but more.

Are you looking back at all of us
    living in our glass terrarium,
laughing on the other side
    of the glass?

13.

ANNA'S RISING

She changes before our eyes
shrinking from large to small.
Like a Russian nesting doll,
her soul chafes against
bone, restless to break out
of her wooden coat.

Her eyes, fading lamps, stare
at the ceiling. Her ribs are bird-cage thin,
her temples blue and concave.
With stick fingers,
she picks at the sheets
ready to pull them overhead.

She lies there all sparrow, tethered
to her bed with her soul hovering above.
I imagine it tied to her body by a strand
of molten glass as the space between
each breath expands. She's beyond
knowing or caring if that thread
should suddenly snap.

Moments after her death,
we see her face still glossed
with light.
Her soul rises,
free at last,
pulled by an unseen cord.

14.

AUTOPSY

The pathologist worked precisely
as a taxidermist or Swiss jeweler.
First, he unzipped the suitcase
of her flesh and opened her
from stem to sternum.
Then he pulled the dead bird
of her heart from its cage
and held it
in his white gloved hand.
He took her two lungs,
hanging like raw fruit
dripping black with tar,
and then the awful offal packed
with globs of yellow fat
stuffed around like rolled socks.

I did not know this woman
with curly gray hair, freckled
from head to toe,
or even her name.
I doubt she imagined
her body would be unpacked
on a cold steel table,
when she sat long ago
slumped in a plush seat
gazing at the silver screen

as Bogart and Bacall blew clouds
in the air, as she sucked life
into a spark that glowed
in the dark like a red beacon
atop a tiny lighthouse,

a vice among others
that wrecked her life.

15.

NO MORE BE GRIEVED

(Dedicated to all who shared their childhood griefs with me.)

Remember how you were a boy
dirt poor from the bayou
and your daddy beat the bejesus
out of you and you were the goat
he pinned his badness on?

Or how you were a girl, trapped
in a rundown trailer as your mother
cried all day then slashed
her battered wrists
and you had to bring up the baby alone?

Or how you were twelve, marched
through blood-filled killing fields,
gripping a hot gun in your cold hands,
forced to aim it at your friends,
your family—and shoot.

Now at the end of your road,
I whisper in your ear,
There is no place to hide,
no place to drop your gripsack
of sorrows, but here.

Let God carry it awhile—
you are so tired now.
You, whose past drags
like a sandbag filled
with regret.

He knows it wasn't your fault.

16.

BLOSSOMING INTO LIGHT

The billows of her spongy lungs
labor to breathe. For a body
about to soar into light, even the air
feels like ballast. Her bones
ache, heavy as steel girders.

She lies by a sun-soaked window
unable to see the yellow wings
of goldfinches—nuggets
of flying butter, flitting and pecking
at the birdfeeders hanging outside.

Three lanterns of plenty
have been hoisted
above her crimson roses.
They sway like wise virgins
lighting her way.

The numbers on her clock
are painted owls, cardinals, and jays.
For her, time always flies. "Something
is wrong with the clock. I can't sleep.
It keeps me awake."

Soon, she will disappear
into a whorl
of goldfinch wings.

17.

GOING HOME TO SPRINGTOWN

This spare cowboy watches his life
seep out slowly
like a slip-line of frayed rope.

Prairie winds stripped and bleached his farm.
Once the pride of Morgan Territory,
his hay barns crumble
like shredded cigars.

All fear burnt out of him
by his hardscrabble life,
he wrestles with the dark wrangler
who rides him till dawn.

His black eyes glow
toward an inscrutable horizon.
He says, "When this is over,
I'm going home to Springtown."

He knows this is so
because his long dead brother
stood by his bed
to show him the way.

He said, "Wouldn't you know,
he's three times smarter
than he used to be."

18.

DYING IS A WILD NIGHT

Death burst into her room,
a savage pit bull
that clamped his greedy jaws
onto her neck
and shook her like a rag doll.

The tumor pressed
inside her brain, sparking
twenty-six seizures in an hour.
All medications tried, two nurses
and I stood helpless. We held
her young body in our arms
as she flailed violently on the bed.

Like the three women
at the foot of the Cross,
it was all we could do
to watch. She was a plane
spiraling out of control, going
down down as if death
was dragging her fast underground.

After she died, we climbed
from beneath the wreckage;
we hugged the family, each other,
and wept. Then we all circled
around her body, at last
serene as snow, and held hands.

I said a trembling prayer,
trusting the words
would touch her soul tenderly,
hoping its balm would heal
the wounds I knew we'd carry
for the rest of our lives.

19.

ODE TO TEX MCKLEAN

At eighty, his boyish grin lopes across his face
after I tell my funny story. Watching it
is better than saying my own punch line.

His eyes, the color of twilight,
contain a luster not bought from moonshine
but daily dips into God's grace.

He said, "I never aimed to be rich,
I'm gonna live till I die, and when I die,
I'm gonna live forever."

He never gets tired of telling
how the Spirit stampeded him once
at an old tent meeting.

His feet danced like tongues of fire that night.
Said he was drunker than a lord,
his body bobbing up and down,

a foot-stomping joy-ride
on the rollercoaster
of God's glory.

Now he prays and waits
as the evening shadows
darken his room.

He hopes for one last burst of grace
before the uncertain ride ahead.

20.

CROSSING THE LINE

Once I knew a man with a wasting disease,
so diminished he shriveled like a praying mantis,
his shrunken brain the size of a grapefruit,
then he curled up and died. The nurse checked—
no heartbeat, no pulse, no breath, nothing.

When his daughter came she cried,
"Oh Dad, I wish I'd been here when you died!"
Suddenly, some unbreakable part of his body
returned and breathed again—love's
utter response to love.

He'd been dying so long, death became
his natural element—at her call,
he surfaced, gulping fresh air. For an hour,
she soothed his brow, held his hand
until, like Lazarus, he died once more.

It makes us feel safe to think the line
between this life and the next
is fixed, hard as adamant, a cliff
pushed up against a black horizon,
a sentence passed by the final Judge.

But just stand at the east and west coasts
of existence and you'll see how this line
is a swinging gate or a curtain,
fluttering in and out an open window.
Sometimes, people slip through.

21.

KADDISH POEM

(For Susan Talon-Mazer RN)

What unnumbered griefs we carry
in our numb hearts—
unuttered sighs, the whispers
of falling leaves.

The Talmud says, "The deeper
the sorrow
the less tongue we have."

Tongue-tied, heart-stung, our deepest griefs
bury themselves alive
in the tombs of our former selves.
Only the welcome lament liberates them.

Let my words be to you
like the green earth cherishing.
Let this song sew up
the tattered seams of your life.

And know, as you bathe
the body of your beloved
with bowls of rain water,
you wash him
with the very tears of God.

22.

ELEGY FOR LYNDSEY

Look how her last three breaths
stopped the world. Everything
you once knew has stalled.
Raindrops hang unfallen
in midair.

Mourning doves fail to sing.
Salmon suspend their yearly run.
Tongues of bells hang mute,
muffled in the waiting belfry
down the street.

I'm here, claiming no grief
as owned by sister, mother, or child,
but simply come as a faithful listener,
a sorrowful priest of the soul.

May my quiet prayer
soothe your heart so newly raw.

May her spirit soar
like white smoke rising
from a snuffed wick,
as she grasps the bliss
of being everywhere.

NOTES

"A Poem for Connor Mclaughlin"
See Justin A. Levine, "Falling Rock Kills 12-year-old Boy at Roaring Brook Falls" (Lake Placid News, Lake Placid, NY, 2016).

"Capel-y-Ffin"
In English this means Chapel of the Boundary. The chapel sits in the Vale of Ewyas in Powys, Wales in a hamlet near the English-Welsh border, two miles north of Llanthony Priory in the Black Mountains. The nearest towns of Clyro and Hay-on-Wye are where the famous Anglican diarist, the Reverend Francis Kilvert (1840–1879), lived and served. The Rev. Joseph Leycester Lyne, known as Father Ignatius of Jesus, founded the first post-Reformation Anglican Benedictine monastery for men in 1863. In 1870, he bought land at Capel-y-Ffin and moved his community to create Llanthony Abbey. On August 30, 1880, after vespers, four choir boys playing in the field saw an apparition of the Virgin Mary. There were three more visions of the Blessed Virgin Mary by ten others, including Fr. Ignatius, for two weeks after this before they ceased. The story goes that soon after these appearances, there was a nun, ill with chronic pain, who doubted the visions were real. Fr. Ignatius gave her some rhubarb leaves touched by the Virgin Mary and she was healed. The monastery at Capel-y-Ffin struggled to retain members until Fr. Ignatius's death in 1908. In 1911, the abbey was given to the Anglican Benedictine monks of Caldey Island. When the Caldey Benedictines collectively submitted to Rome in 1913, Llanthony Abbey was later sold to the writer, sculptor, and typographer, Eric Gill, who started an artist's colony there from 1924 to 1928. Since 1972, there has been a yearly ecumenical

pilgrimage from Capel-y-Ffin church to the abbey to mark the anniversary of the apparitions with evensong and a Eucharist.

"St. Francis Xavier Mission Kahnawake, 2019"
Saint Kateri Tekakwitha (1656–1680) was born an Algonquin-Mohawk. She was beatified by Pope John Paul II in 1980 and canonized by Pope Benedict XVI at Saint Peter's Basilica on October 21, 2012. She is the patron saint of ecologists and the environment.

AUTHOR BIOGRAPHY

Pamela Cranston was born in New York City and raised in Deerfield, Massachusetts. She studied Russian history and journalism at Stetson University from 1968 to 1971, where she was editor of *The Reporter*, the school's weekly newspaper.

In 1974, she traveled to Somerset, England, to become the first American to join the Community of St. Francis (CSF)—Franciscan first order nuns in the Anglican Communion associated with the Society of St. Francis (SSF). Later, she transferred to the first American CSF house in San Francisco. While there in community, she worked on skid row, volunteered as chaplain at San Francisco County jail, served the homeless through the Catholic Worker, and helped Latina refugees. After leaving the order in 1978, she helped start the Episcopal Sanctuary for the homeless in San Francisco and worked in the alcoholism recovery field as a counselor and administrator for the San Francisco Public Health Department.

In 1984, she received a Bachelor of Arts degree from San Francisco State University in inter-disciplinary social science, gerontology, and creative writing. In 1988 she received a Master of Divinity degree, with distinction, from the Church Divinity School of the Pacific (CDSP) in Berkeley, California. Ordained as an Episcopal priest in 1990, she has served several San Francisco Bay area churches and hospices for the past thirty-three years.

Her books include a novel, *The Madonna Murders* (St. Huberts, 2003), *Coming to Treeline: Adirondack Poems* (St. Huberts, 2005), and *Searching for Nova Albion* (Wipf and Stock, 2019). Her poems, essays, and book reviews have appeared in numerous books and journals: *Adirondack Review, Anglican Theological Review, Blueline Anthology* (Syracuse University Press), *Crosswinds Poetry Journal, Mystic River Review, Naugatuck River Review, Penwood Review, The Sow's Ear Poetry Review, The Windhover,* and many other publications.

Searching for Nova Albion was a semi-finalist winner in the 2020 Poetry Society of Virginia North American Poetry Contest. Her poem "My Grandfather's Typewriter" won fifth place in the 2020 Writer's Digest Poetry Awards. Her poem "The House of Metaphor" won honorable mention for the Poetry Society of Virginia 2021 Edgar Allan Poe Memorial Prize.

Pamela lives with her husband, Edward, in Oakland, California.